A BOOK FOR WOMEN AND THE MEN WHO LOVE THEM

BREAK THE ICE

"YOU, ME, US"

DAWSON CLARK

TABLE OF CONTENT

INTRODUCTION

Relationships are a lot like a video game. You can have all the best gear and skills, but if you don't know how to play the game, nothing will work out well for you.

Think about it: when you're playing a video game, what do you need to know? That's right—you need to know how to play! You need to know how to read your opponent's moves, anticipate their next move, and adapt your own strategy accordingly. If you don't understand these basic concepts, then the game isn't going anywhere fast—and neither is your relationship.

So what does this have to do with relationships? Well, understanding how people communicate with each other is key to understanding how they communicate in general. So if we want our relationships to grow and flourish—and they are no exception! —then we need to learn how people communicate with each other! And that starts with being empathetic listeners who can get inside their partners' heads and feel what they're feeling.

It's not all about "YOU" or "ME", neither is it about "US" but it's all about "YOU", "ME" and how it affects "US".

PART 1

LISTEN TO HER

Have you ever noticed, how without a word, that some people make you feel justified and understood? What is it about them that makes it so easy for you to open up and share your struggles? They are the people you turn to when you need to talk about your feelings and needs.

The answer is simple - listening empathically will help you understand and communicate with others more effectively. That's why they make such great conversation partners. They're the perfect people to talk to because everyone else seems to gravitate towards them. They are good friends with everyone in the office and have a strong connection with everyone they meet. If you're not familiar with the term "empathic listening," it's a skill that can be developed with practice and repetition. This is going to lead to the expected results.

What Is Empathic Listening?

The goal of empathic listening is to hear your conversation partner as they truly are. It is being able to listen attentively and with an open mind to other people's thoughts and beliefs.

Empathic listening allows you to become attuned to your partner's emotional frequencies and to resonate with them on an emotional level. Listening attentively opens up a channel to the innermost thoughts and feelings of the person being listened to, creating a safe space where they can share anything without feeling judged or criticized. When empathy is the bridge that holds two people together, words become less important and more important is the relationship between them.

THE ANSWER IS SIMPLE

Listening empathically will help you understand and communicate with others more effectively.

Being empathetic doesn't mean you have to agree with everything, and it doesn't mean you have to do anything on their behalf. It's not difficult to understand other people's perspectives; we just need to take a step back and try to see things from their perspective. Sadly, not all people are born empaths. Not everyone can easily identify, process, and empathize with the emotions of others. We can develop and improve this skill through patience and exercise. If you find it difficult to feel your own emotions, learning to improve empathy may not be as difficult as you think. Any ability can be learned, as long as you are motivated and willing to take the necessary steps to practice it.

Empathy: The Key to Authentic Human Interactions.

Many people in today's world are running after things, which makes it difficult for them to be patient and listen to others. This has led to a situation in which many people are speaking without thinking, which can cause problems. We believe that others will understand us without ever having to put ourselves in their shoes. We want others to share our views without giving them the opportunity to voice their opinions. We seldom respond to others' opinions or compliments, even if they are offered.

Our interactions become superficial and unemotional because we don't really connect with each other. It's not necessary for things to be this way. If you are willing to listen rather than speak, understand rather than criticize, and comfort rather than judge, you can quickly turn the conversation into true human interaction, whether you are talking to your spouse, friend, boss, co-worker, neighbor, or even the coffee maker who Running at your favorite coffee shop, emotional listening can dramatically improve the quality of your interaction. Contrary to popular belief, it was cooperation, not competition, that helped mankind survive, prosper and achieve the level of socio-economic development that we are seeing today.

What is The Relationship Between Empathy and Happiness?

Some of you'll be questioning how precisely does taking note of others and seeking to resonate emotionally with them make contributions to our well-being. What does empathic listening must do with happiness? First of all, empathetic ears are tough to return back through those days. Many humans are too self-concerned to care approximately what others must say. But for the reason that wholesome social interactions are vital to our growth, understanding how empathize is one of the elements of a glad and enjoyable life. Research indicates that whilst you concentrate in an empathic manner, humans are happy with the communication and also you right away grow to be

"There is a clear distinction between listening and looking ahead for your opportunity to speak."

extra socially attractive. And considering that we're all social creatures through nature, being capable of navigate social conditions efficaciously will in a roundabout way make contributions to our average experience of happiness and well-being.

Finally, for the reason that empathic listeners are social magnets, they frequently gain from thrilling possibilities that make contributions to their non-public and expert growth. Overall, empathic listening can substantially make contributions to our standard experience of happiness and well-being.

"There is a clear distinction between listening and looking ahead for your opportunity to speak."

Empathic Listening for Couples

Empathic conversation is a crucial element of any successful and lasting relationship. The capacity to be empathetically closer to the one you love has large results on the general degree of delight you and your partner revel in for your relationship. As you could imagine, understanding a way to pay attention with an open mind - without interruptions, criticism, and undesirable advice - is a 'must' in any healthful and useful couple. Too often, those who deeply love themselves turn out to be splitting due to conversation issues. Whether it manifests as stonewalling, criticism, or contempt, loss of empathy can slowly flip human beings into strangers who resent every different. And that's due to the fact one in every of our essential wishes is to be heard and understood. When this doesn't happen, you start to sense lonely and abandoned. You go through and in the end distance yourself, even from someone you cherished extra than you can ever imagine. Empathic listening paves the manner for affectionate verbal exchange, a critical detail for any healthful couple.

When empathic listening turns into a dependency that characterizes your relationship, you could without difficulty resonate together along with your partner's struggles and recognize why he/she is probably feeling that way. And this offers you the opportunity to discover answers seal the 'cracks' that would compromise your relationship.

All and all, empathic listening builds robust relationships, fosters powerful communications, and cultivates agreement with among existence partners.

PART 2

REALLY SEE HER

If you've been in a relationship for a prolonged period of time, you already know that loving relationship isn't approximately steady butterflies and sparks. You fall right into a recurring cycle and matters can end up mundane or cyclical to no one's fault. As your dating evolves, much less time is spent on drooling on one another. It will become greater about making life manifest and handling our busy schedules. The routinization of our day by day lives could make us under-recognize our significant other. Making an attempt to bring the intensity of what you sense can convey you again to the honeymoon section of the connection and save you possible lifetime resentment, emotions of neglect, or distance. While it is crucial to bear in mind now no longer to push or rush a connection, there are a few approaches you may sense in the direction of your associate and cause them to feel cherished without forcing matters along. Believe it or not, making small changes to foster a newfound love or closeness can convey you collectively in a manner you could not have experienced before.

" Don't expect easy hints are sufficient to hold your connection alive"

All relationships require plenty of attempt and protection so as for it to achieve success including short- and long-term; however, there are a few little hints to assist develop that intensity and connection, wherein you could enlarge those emotions of affection and preserve the once fluttering wings flapping for your stomach. Of course, love calls for consistent time and interest to hold it going. Once you decide to date, continuous work and care continues to be put in thereafter. Don't expect easy hints are sufficient to hold your connection alive. However, so long as you maintain strengthening your relationship and sharing that love in a reciprocal manner, you are certain to have a better chance of working out within side the long run. Here are 12 thoughts on a way to make a person sense cherished and deepen your connection, in keeping with your relationship.

1

Follow Through with Promises

Make your companion feel cherished via way of means of following through in your promises. If a person can believe you, they likely will experience extra snug having the love connection you share flow ahead. Trust is a massive a part of why relationships flow ahead or why they wreck. If you display you are dependable and can be there whenever needed, it's going to allow your partner experience that more closeness and confirmation. It ought not to be grand gestures or shows of trust, either — simply consistent follow-through to your commitments to each other which can appear small within side the moment, however add to a far larger, more potent relationship.

2

Do A Small Act of Kindness

very little gestures that ease your partner's life show a great deal for how much you care. Whether or not it's packing your [significant other] a lunch before they burst forth to a busy day of work, or stopping by the mall to choose up a phone case for your [partner] to avoid wasting [them] a visit — these are the sorts of non-verbal actions that show you're deeply endowed in this relationship, and seeking active ways that make your partner's life better. It very profound that it is the smaller gestures that count; even one thing like asking if you'll be able to pick up dinner for them on the way home, or creating a fast call to assist them schedule an appointment, could be a nice reminder that there is somebody in their corner.

3

Spend Quality Time Together

Whether or not it's making plans for weekly date nights or having an outing together, constantly carve out time to be with one other. And while you are spending that pleasant time together, allow matters go with the drift naturally and provide your companion your undivided attention. Spend time viewing a movie together and [don't] take a look at your cellphone or email. Show your partner that you want to be a valued part of their company and make this a normal culture.

4

Give A Passionate Kiss

When in the spur of the moment, kissing is usually an excellent idea – given you've got your companion's consent, of course. Looking deeply and passionately into their eyes as you kiss them is a superb way to create and build connection. So regularly we go along with the drift and kisses are only a little percent right here or there. But in case you take a second to attempt to be a great kisser and deepen that kiss, your partner will without a doubt notice.

5

Make Eye Contact

Make eye contact to make a person sense being loved. Show appreciation and passion through maintaining eye contact. When you take some time to mirror upon and deepen the gratitude you experience toward your partner, they could sense it. It's nearly like a 'vibe' you radiate, and it may be conveyed within-side the excellence of your touch, or maybe in the way in that you make eye contact. Additionally, research has confirmed that the mere act of eye contact evokes its very own type of intimacy – that the instant eyes connect, it triggers an exhilarating experience for the opposite person's state of mind as an person, and vice versa. Taking the time to observe in with one another on this quick, nonverbal gesture is an open way to help anticipate every one's expectations and needs, and assist to hold an open communication path between yourselves.

6

Be Present in The Moment

Making your partner feel cherished is all about being with them totally and utterly – no words needed. once you have been with somebody for a while, it is easy to be in a rut. however, if you're taking the time to disconnect from your phone or any outside distractions, your partner can feel a bigger association knowing you are being completely present with them.

7

Touch Them More

Although physical touch is not your love language, attempt a tender (consensual!) touch or caress to bring you nearer to your partner. Or, if you are both game, perhaps even try a massage. Receiving a massage has been shown to raise levels of oxytocin, the brain chemical that bonds two individuals together. So, if you wish your partner to fall a lot more deeply in love, extended physical touch can do the trick."

8

Recreate Your First Date

Bringing back sweet nostalgic memories can prompt you both of the feelings you had once you first fell for one another. attempt to incorporate any very little details that may be a reminder in successive days of your night. Undoubtedly dress up, have a similar or same meal, add candlelight, be extra. It's not simply nostalgic of the start of your relationship; it conjointly brings you back thereto 'this is why I fell crazy with you' [feeling].].

9

Listen To Them

Make your girlfriend or lover feel special by listening. If you wish to understand a way to make your partner feel special, provide them your undivided attention. Being a superb listener to your partner may be a great way help them feel appreciated. you don't have to be compelled to say a word or try and fix any problems, however lending a listening ear will go an extended way to make your partner fall deeper infatuated with you as a result of they feel heard.

10

Make Them a Thank You Card

Expressing gratitude in your relationship is crucial; it's a significant player in deciding matrimonial quality. Offer your partner a physical card with a personalised message from you. purchase one, create one, as long as you'll be able to surprise them with a novel reminder of what they mean to you. Once you've written your message, place it in their laptop, bag, notebook, or any item that they regularly use.

11

Figure Out and Understand Their Love Language

Trying to understand out a way to make your girlfriend or wife feel cherished? Figure out and understand their love language. According to the author - Dr. Gary Chapman, there are 5 love languages – words of affirmation, acts of service, receiving gifts, pleasant time, and bodily touch – that we use to specifically display and recognize love. Everyone has a love language in phrases of the way they talk in romantic relationships and what they desire, or on the very least, sure styles of love languages they will reply to greater than others. So, be aware of what your companion's talking about and the way you could assist one other. Find out what form of love language they have, and ensure to handle issues with a view to lead them to happiness and satisfaction.

12

Take an Impromptu Road Trip

Not solely is it spontaneous, that helps keep the tingly feeling alive, however it's also the simplest way to make a really intimate emotional atmosphere (car talks are forever the deepest). Hop within the car, shut down the GPS, and drive aimlessly. Most of the time we tend to neglect our darling ones as a result, we are therefore immersed in ourselves and our routines. Driving in conjunction with no destination in mind helps you wish to lose yourselves in new experiences, to check your ability to handle the world, and therefore the strength of your union in navigating through unknowns together.

PART 3

THE REALITY

Your partner comes home all worked up. Their boss undermined them at work again; they rant approximately how terrible it feels by no means not to be recognized. But one issue results in some other and all a sudden, you're both in a fight.

"How did the tables flip so fast?"

What would possibly have commenced as your partner blowing off steam speedy changed into a conflict among you two. But, possibilities are, that didn't simply happen. In fact, you're both at fault here. While your partner won't be withinside the clear, you most probably had been responsible of one factor: loss of empathy. You would possibly assume listening is sufficient whilst your partner is upset. But displaying you recognize how your partner is feeling and that you're there to pay attention is even extra important.

"Empathy is what really matters once your partner is talking concerning their struggles"

A study conducted by researchers at the University of California Berkley. Participants in a very intimate relationship were asked to log their arguments daily, rating how understood and happy they felt in their relationship after. They found that couples that understood one another better throughout an argument thought more highly of their relationships. In fact, just the straightforward act of one partner making an attempt to grasp the opposite made the person feel happier. Therefore, whereas listening is the opening move for communication during a relationship, empathy is what really matters once your partner is talking concerning their struggles.

However, that doesn't come easily for everyone. you'll be thinking, "I invariably say and do the incorrect things!" and that i completely feel that as a result of I'm accustomed be the same, I struggled to seek out the proper words; I felt like everything I aforementioned made things with my partner worse. However, empathy isn't one thing you need to be born with; it's one thing you'll be able to learn and practice. If you would like to work towards helping your partner feel a lot of understood and heard, give these concepts a try.

Be close to them

Taking note of your partner from another space will come back off as uncaring. Physical closeness establishes an affiliation that says you're there and listening. Sit down next to your partner as they relay to you what's going on. produce a peaceful area for your partner to be there next to you. If they're hospitable physical touch, hold their hand throughout your conversation. offer your partner a hug if they appear overwhelmed. an easy act of touch can show what proportion you understand their distress.

Don't be quick to advice

I'm positive each single one amongst you'll be able to think about a time wherever you were talking to someone about a problem, and that they jumped in with unwarranted advice. I do know this is often a private complaint of mine. Here's a bit of stories that may get you so much in life: most of the time, folks just wish to vent. particularly if that person could be a friend, partner, or family, they simply have to be compelled to say things. They don't expect you to possess the answers. Therefore, take the pressure off yourself to have the solution; your partner doesn't expect that hefty role of you.

Validate their feelings

rather than giving advice, choose to validate their feelings. If they're coming back to you feeling emotionally} drained due to however alarming their boss treats them, be with them at that moment. Acknowledge that it is sensible they feel that manner as a result, it sounds exhausting to you as well. an easy “I can see you’re very upset” or “I perceive how that might be frustrating” lets your partner recognize you honor the way they’re feeling. validating their feelings doesn’t mean you agree. However, what your partner feels could be a fact. whether or not you agree or not doesn’t mean they don’t feel that emotion wholly.

Put Down Your Phone

Nobody goes to assume you’re taking note of them if your eyes are affixed to your phone. consider the last time you had a very important oral communication with someone. However, would you have felt if they'd picked up their phone while you talked about your struggles? place down your phone pay close attention to your partner. provide them your undivided attention. If you don’t follow this step, the remainder won’t necessarily matter. you would like to actively hear what your partner is saying. That won’t happen together with your Instagram feed in your hand.

Ask Questions for Clarification

If one thing your partner says doesn't add up to you, don't nod and allow them to continue. a part of actively listening is asking questions for clarification. Therefore, if your partner appears like they were "undermined," ask them in what ways that they felt that. Tell them to explain to you what being undermined feels like. Asking questions not solely helps you perceive your partner's state of affairs better it however lets them see you care enough to engage.

CONCLUSION

Breaking the ice when communicating with your partner transcends beyond just listening. It's all about **"YOU, ME** and **US"**

Understanding how intertwined these three personalities are connected throughout a relationship is vital to the shared sustainability coexisting within the relationship. In essence what **"YOU"** do affects **"ME"** which ultimately affects **"US"**.

So, go live and experience a positively transformed relationship.

www.ingramcontent.com/pod-product-compliance
Lightning Source LLC
LaVergne TN
LVHW010511160826
845677LV00012B/2796

* 9 7 9 8 3 5 3 3 3 4 2 8 6 *